SO-AGI-312

DICK RUTAN & JEANA YEAGER

FLYING NON-STOP AROUND THE WORLD

BY

Laurie Rozakis

Illustrations by Jerry Harston

A BLACKBIRCH PRESS BOOK

WOODBRIDGE, CONNECTICUT

Published by Blackbirch Press, Inc.
One Bradley Road
Woodbridge , CT 06525

©1994 Blackbirch Press, Inc.
First Edition

All rights reserved. No part of this book may be reproduced in any form without permission in writing from Blackbirch Press, Inc., except by a reviewer.

Printed in Hong Kong

10 9 8 7 6 5 4 3 2 1

Library of Congress Cataloging-in-Publication Data

Rozakis, Laurie.
    Jeana Yeager & Dick Rutan, flying non-stop around the world / by Laurie Rozakis. —1st ed.
        p.   cm. — (Partners)
    Includes bibliographical references and index.
    ISBN 1-56711-087-8   ISBN 1-56711-118-1 (Pbk.)
    1. Voyager (Airplane)—Juvenile literature. 2. Rutan, Dick—Journeys—Juvenile literature. 3. Yeager, Jeana—Journeys—Juvenile literature. 4. Flights around the world—Juvenile literature. [1. Voyager (Airplane). 2. Rutan, Dick. 3. Yeager, Jeana. 4. Flights around the world.] I. Title. II. Title: Jeana Yeager and Dick Rutan, flying non-stop around the world. III. Series.
G445.R69 1994
629.13'09—dc20
                                                    94-20399
                                                      CIP
                                                      AC

~ Contents ~

In 1986, Dick Rutan and Jeana
Yeager made history by flying
around the world without stopping.

— ▌ —

Up, Up, and Away!

It was Tuesday, December 23, 1986. Tens of thousands of people crowded around a dry desert lake bed, staring into the clear blue sky. Around the world, millions more people were glued to the news programs on their television sets. Everyone was hoping that history would be made. It was that day that two adventurers named Jeana Yeager and Dick Rutan tried to become the first people to fly around the world without stopping or refueling. They had been in the air for nine long days and nights. "This is probably more demanding than any flight that has ever been done," said the former head of the Smithsonian Institution's Air and Space Museum.

Aiming for a New World's Record

Today, the longest non-stop commercial airplane flights are 7,475 miles. This is the distance from San Francisco, California, to Sydney, Australia. Airplane companies are now working on building an airplane that can travel 9,000 miles without stopping to refuel. Before Dick and Jeana's trip, the farthest an airplane had ever traveled on one load of fuel was 12,532 miles, a record set by two Air Force pilots in 1962. They flew in a B-52 bomber plane that had been specially redesigned to hold more fuel.

It is nearly 26,000 miles around the world. In 1986, Dick Rutan and Jeana Yeager were trying to fly 13,468 miles further than had ever been flown without stopping for fuel. Since there was no airplane already in existence that could do this, Dick, Jeana, and their friends and family had built their own craft: the H-shaped *Voyager*. Empty, it weighs 938 pounds and has a wingspan of 111 feet. It is able to fly—unassisted by air currents—about 100 miles per hour. Dick and Jeana were flying a brand new airplane, a one-of-a-kind. Even

To achieve their goal, Dick and Jeana designed their own special aircraft.

with the test flights, no one knew how the *Voyager* would perform on such a long, dangerous flight.

Inside, *Voyager* is tiny: three-and-a-half feet wide by seven feet long. Burt Rutan, Dick's brother, calls it "a telephone booth on its side." Since the *Voyager* is so small, it cannot carry all the backup radios, radar, and other parts found on other airplanes. That meant, on their journey, Jeana and Dick were soaring over vast stretches of ocean, mountains, and plains entirely on their own.

The plane's size and shape presents other challenges, too. Imagine tossing and turning in a rowboat on the high seas. It's bumpy! That's what it feels like to travel in the super-lightweight *Voyager.*

First, Further, and Faster

Most of us see and hear airplanes nearly every day. As a result, we don't think too much of the wonders of flight. But the history of aviation, or air flight, is actually very short—only a hundred years long!

On December 17, 1903, Wilbur and Orville Wright made the first successful airplane flight. The plane, called *Flyer I,* stayed in the air for 12 seconds. The longest flight the Wright brothers made lasted 59 seconds and covered 852 feet. Twenty-four years later, Charles A. Lindbergh became the first person in history to fly alone across the Atlantic Ocean. It took Lindbergh 33 hours and 32 minutes to fly from Long Island, New York, to Paris, France—a total distance of 3,610 miles. He called his airplane the *Spirit of St. Louis.* In 1932, Amelia Earhart piloted her small airplane from Newfoundland to Ireland, becoming the first woman to cross the Atlantic. Five years later, she tried to circle the globe over the Pacific Ocean, but she disappeared somewhere near Hawaii. Despite years of careful searching and investigating, no trace of her airplane has ever been found. Other air pioneers, however, were luckier.

The first successful airplane flight was made by the Wright brothers in 1903.

In October 1947, Chuck Yeager (no relation to Jeana), was the first person in aviation history to fly faster than the speed of sound (which is also referred to as the Mach number). His top speed was 967 miles per hour. On July 28, 1976, Captain Eldon W. Joersz and Major George T. Morgan, Jr. set the world's speed record when they flew 2,193 miles per hour.

Terrifying Risks

In December 1986, Jeana and Dick sat in their aircraft and focused on the dangerous journey they were about to take. They were thinking about only one thing: surviving the trip.

"You are cleared for take-off," the tower crew's words crackled over *Voyager*'s radio. Jeana and Dick knew they faced many great obstacles. Nearly ninety-five percent of the trip would be over water. Would the *Voyager* be torn apart in a wild ocean storm? Would Jeana and Dick lose their way in a dense, black thundercloud? Would the small airplane smash into a mountain in a fiery ball of flame? Nobody knew the answers to these questions.

Jeana and Dick knew they faced many great obstacles but decided their goal was worth the risk.

And what about rest and food? Only 22 pounds of food and 10.5 gallons of water could fit into *Voyager*. After a four-and-a-half day test flight, Jeana had fainted because she hadn't had enough water. Could they go more than a week on peanut-butter-crunch energy bars, other dried foods, and only one real meal a day? And then there was the problem of thunderous noise.

The airplane's body was so thin that the engine's earsplitting roar could not be blocked out. To cut down on extra weight, Jeana and Dick did not put sound insulation in *Voyager*. They had earphones, but these only blocked out part of the engine's deafening roar.

Everyone was also worried about the possible effects of the high altitude. The higher one flies, the less oxygen is in the air. Flying at 8,000 to 12,000 feet—*Voyager*'s cruising altitude—without enough oxygen can make people very sick. When the human body is deprived of oxygen, the brain begins to swell and fluid fills the lungs. To save space and weight, Dick and Jeana could only carry a small supply of extra oxygen. If they ran out, they would surely not be able to survive the flight.

Despite all the dangers and the potential problems, Jeana Yeager and Dick Rutan were determined to make their journey. They both felt that achieving their historic goal would make all their hardships and troubles seem worthwhile. And even though they were not sure at any point that they would succeed, both were going to give it the best try they possibly could.

2

Dick Rutan

Dick Rutan first fell in love when he was just a young boy in the 10th grade. "I took one look and I was hooked," he later recalled. His love? The "Super Sabre," the Air Force's F-100 fighter plane! "I knew right away that what I most wanted in life was to fly one of them," he now remembers.

Dreams of Flying

Dick dreamed of flying from the time he could walk. Neither of his parents were fliers—his father was a dentist and his mother was a homemaker. But the Rutans understood what flying meant to Dick and to

Dick dreamed of flying from the time he could walk. As a child, he often built model planes and "flew" them at home-made "airports" in his backyard.

his younger brother, Burt. They helped Dick and Burt reach for the sky. The Rutans took their sons to air shows all over California. By the time Dick was four years old, he was building airports in his yard between the fruit trees. Soon Dick was building model airplanes to land in his airports. "Dick would build a model," his mother remembers, "and when an accident happened, Burt would take Dick's broken airplanes and redesign them into something he wanted to fly—and they would fly."

Dick was always glad to have his brother's help, because he wanted to fly even more than he wanted to build airplanes. By the time he was a teenager, he was going to air shows on his own. For hours, he stood in the wide open fields and stared up at the fighter pilots in their planes. "To me, they were like superheroes." Dick later said.

"The Velvet Arm"

Dick took his first flying lessons when he was just 15 years old. To raise money to pay for the costly lessons, he picked grapes and carried trays of raisins in nearby orchards. His first solo flight came after just five-and-a-half hours of training, stretched out

As soon as he was a teenager, Dick went to air shows on his own.

over six months. By the time he was 16, he had already earned his flying license. That meant he could fly an airplane before he could drive a car! Dick then went on to earn commercial, instrument, multiengine, seaplane, and instructor licenses.

Young Dick took a lot of pride in his flying skills and appearance. He started to call himself "the Velvet Arm" after some bodybuilders he knew. But he was so skinny that everyone called him "Pretzel" instead!

Into the Air Force

In high school, Dick realized that he actually could become a pilot. The dream was within his reach. As soon as he could, Dick signed on to train in the Air Force air cadet program. Unfortunately, he had been so busy flying that he had not done much school work. Dick failed the Air Force written test and could not enter pilot's school, so he signed on as a navigator instead. It was not until 1966 that Dick got into the pilot training program. By this time, almost seven years had passed.

Dick had been waiting for this chance for his whole life. Soon, he was at the top of his class.

As a result, he finally got his shot at flying his dream plane, the F-100. In 1967, he was assigned to fight in the Vietnam War.

Hero in Vietnam

The Vietnam War lasted from 1959 to 1975. The war began when the North Vietnamese and the Vietcong—Communist troops—tried to overthrow the democratic government of South Vietnam. The struggle became a war between North and South Vietnam. The United States and 40 other countries supported South Vietnam by sending troops and weapons. The Soviet Union and China supported the Vietcong in North Vietnam. In 1969, at the height of the war, America had 541,000 soldiers fighting in this bloody battle.

Dick signed up with the U.S. Air Force's famous Commando Sabre outfit, code name "Misty." These pilots swept low over North Vietnam to bomb supplies that were being ferried across rivers on boats. They also attacked convoys, aircraft sites, and supply depots. The pilots marked the targets with smoke rockets and then called in circling fighter bombers for the actual attacks.

After hundreds of dangerous flying missions in the Vietnam War, Dick's plane was shot down over the South China Sea.

Attack!

The Commando Sabre missions were so dangerous
that most pilots stayed only four months with the
Misty unit. But Dick signed up for a second, and
then a third, tour of duty. On his 105th mission,
Dick was flying over the jungle when he heard a
noise like someone hammering the bottom of his
plane with a bat. He was hit and his plane was in
flames! "I must make it to the ocean," he thought.
With all the flying skill he could come up with, Dick
steered the flaming airplane to the South China Sea.
Once he was over water, he bailed out, tugged his
parachute cord, and splashed into the ocean. Three
hours later, he was rescued, unharmed. In total,
Dick had flown an incredible 325 combat missions
in the Vietnam War.

Soon after his rescue, he was shipped to Italy,
and in 1975, he landed back home. After he had
served 20 years in the Air Force, Dick felt it was
time to move on. He left the armed forces and
decided to become a test pilot for his brother Burt's
airplane company. Little did he know what the
future—and a certain 97-pound girl from Texas—
held in store for him!

~ 3 ~

Jeana Yeager

Most babies ask for "mama" or a "bottle" when they first learn to speak. Not Jeana Yeager. Her first sentence was "I want a horse!" By the time she was three years old, she had her first horse. Jeana was very little and the horse was very big. It was so big, in fact, that Jeana could walk under it without bending her head! Of course, Jeana could not get on the horse by herself. "Wait for us to help you," her parents would call. "I am going to get on that horse myself!" Jeana would reply. Then she would lead the horse to a wooden picnic table, climb up on top, and jump on to the horse's back. That's when Jeana's parents first knew their daughter would be able to do anything in life.

Run Like the Wind

One of the things Jeana most loved as a child was running. By the time she was in high school, she had become one of Texas's best track-and-field stars.

In 1970, when the starter's pistol fired for the Texas state finals, Jeana was off like a shot, racing down the track. As her arms and legs pumped furiously, she strained every muscle in her body. The crowd roared! It was the most important race she had ever run. Jeana loved the strong, free feeling she got from running. She liked to feel the wind whipping through her long brown hair. Most of the other racers were bigger and stronger, and some were older, too. How could little Jeana win against them? She tried by using every ounce of strength she had. Besides, winning or losing was not first in her mind. Jeana Yeager just liked to push herself.

Jeana pushed herself harder and harder, straining to get a breath into her lungs. With a final burst of energy, she crossed the finish line. Jeana had won her first medal! She won a lot more medals in her racing career, but she was most proud of this one because she had pushed to the limit and had outrun bigger, stronger, and older girls.

In 1970, Jeana won the Texas state track-and-field finals by beating older girls who were stronger and bigger than she was.

Aim for the Stars

In 1972, two years after Jeana graduated from high school, she married Jon Anthony Farrar. He was a police officer in Texas, where Jeana and her family lived. Jon was loving and kind, and at first they were happy together. But after five years, Jeana became restless. She wanted more adventure and excitement in her life, and she wanted to feel more of a purpose for living. So, she packed up her clothes in a large suitcase, headed to Santa Rosa, California, and moved in with her older sister Judy. Once she was on her own, Jeana was very sad about hurting her husband, but she knew that she had to take charge of her life and begin a new direction. Jeana had always been very good in art. With those skills, she got a job drafting and surveying for an energy company. In the meantime, she and her husband officially got a divorce.

After five years of marriage, Jeana decided her life needed to take a new and more exciting direction.

After a short while in California, Jeana's spirit of adventure took over, and she decided to learn to fly airplanes. By 1978, she had earned her wings. And by 1986, Jeana had set nine speed-and-endurance records for flying. From there, it was only a short leap to skydiving. Soon, she was an expert in that, too. One day, she heard about a man who was building a rocket in his garage. Jeana decided to visit him.

The man was Robert Truax. He had been a captain in the U.S. Navy and knew a lot about rockets. Among his biggest projects were helping to design the rockets that were used to break the sound barrier and inventing launching pads for rockets at sea. Jeana went to work for Bob, making drawings of the rockets. Soon, she learned all about rockets and engineering. Bob knew that Jeana was very smart and brave and could do anything she set her mind to—even fly a rocket into space. "This is Jeana," he would always say, "she's my astronaut."

Finding Each Other

One day in 1980, Jeana went to an air show in Chino, California. She wanted to see all the airplane displays and watch the test planes do loops and stunts in the sky. As she strolled through the field, she stopped at the Rutan Aircraft display. The whole

In 1980, Jeana met Dick at an airshow in Chino, California. They spoke all afternoon about planes and flying.

Rutan family was there—Burt, Mom, Pop, Mike and Sally Melvill, and Dick. Jeana spoke to Dick all afternoon. At the end of the day, she knew that she had not seen the last of this interesting and energetic pilot.

Sure enough, Dick called her the next weekend. Jeana started to come down to the Rutan Aircraft factory on weekends where she would help build wild new airplanes. During those weekends, Dick and Jeana found that they had a lot in common. They both looked for challenges and worked hard. Their interests drew them together, and soon they fell deeply in love. By the end of the year, Dick talked Jeana into coming down to Mojave, California with him.

During their weekends together at the Rutan Aircraft factory, Dick and Jeana found they had a lot in common. Soon, they fell in love.

In 1981, Dick decided to quit his job as chief test pilot at the Rutan Aircraft factory. Soon after that, Dick and Jeana decided to start their own company. Before they began work, they went to lunch with Burt Rutan at the Mojave Inn. They didn't realize it then, but it was a lunch that would soon help them to make history.

━ 4 ━

From Design to Runway

In 1981, Jeana, Dick, and Burt sat at lunch at the Mojave Inn.

"How can we get everyone excited about our new company?" Dick wondered aloud.

"I don't know," his brother answered. "But I have been doing a lot of work with light, super-strong aircraft materials."

"New materials," Jeana said slowly. Then an idea came to her. "We could use them to build an airplane that could break the record for flying around the world without stopping or refueling."

Dick and Jeana decided at that moment that they were going to be the first to try to circle the globe on one tank of gas.

The previous record—set in 1962 by a B-52 bomber—was 12,532 miles. Burt told them that he could easily build a plane that could fly twice as far. He even drew a picture of his dream plane on a napkin right there at the lunch table!

Getting Started

At lunch, Burt had made building the airplane sound simple, but it was far from a snap. Dick, Burt, and Jeana had to build a very light airplane that could carry two people, lots of equipment, and a very heavy load of fuel—nearly 10,000 pounds of gasoline. It took over five years of long, hard work to get the plane from the small, rough sketch on the napkin to the runway.

Jeana and Dick rented a shed at Mojave Airport for $65 a month. Their friends and family pitched in, spending all their time and much of their money on the dream. They worked 12 hours a day, 7 days a week. They worked until they could not stand up anymore. Dick's mother brought bags of food to her son and Jeana, because she knew that if she didn't supply them with nourishment, neither one would remember to eat!

Dick and Jeana built the *Voyager* in a rented shed in the Mojave Desert. They worked night and day for nearly four years to complete it.

The first problem for the team was money: An airplane like the one they needed would cost a fortune—more than a million dollars! Dick and Jeana called many wealthy people and large companies to see if any would give them money. "Your dream is impossible," was the common response. "We won't give you any money for such a crazy idea." But some people without a lot of money did believe in *Voyager*. Dick formed a club that he called "V.I.P.— *Voyager* Impressive People" Club. One man even sent his lunch money and a kind note saying that he was sorry he could not give more.

Because Burt Rutan was a famous aircraft builder, many airplane companies donated costly equipment, such as the rear engine and material for the body. These would have cost hundreds of thousands of dollars. To raise more money, Dick and Jeana sold souvenirs, too. Many people bought little models of *Voyager* for $20.

In the Home Stretch

Dick and Burt built a special oven that they needed to make the material for *Voyager's* body. No one had ever made this material before. After many months of tireless work, they finally got the oven to heat to a steady 3,000 degrees Fahrenheit. That's six times hotter than the hottest home oven!

Then they had to sand the body. Dick alone wore out four pairs of gloves just sanding *Voyager*. Finally, by 1984, their dream aircraft was just about done. It had cost $2 million in parts and had taken nearly four years to complete. When they were done, however, Dick, Jeana, and Burt truly had an airplane of the future.

The completed *Voyager* looked like a cross between a seagull and a flying dinosaur. Even though it was made of many space-age materials and had a futuristic shape, the basic design was nearly the same one used by the Wright brothers way back in 1903!

By 1984, the dream plane was almost done. It had cost $2 million in parts and had taken nearly four years to complete.

The plane's H-shape, called a "canard" shape, put the main wing in the back. This creates a very stable frame and strong wings. (*Voyager*'s wings are 111 feet long, longer than the wings on a 727 jet. It has 17 fuel tanks, but empty, it weighs just 938 pounds!)

Test Flights

By 1986, at long last, *Voyager* was ready for flight. In July, Jeana and Dick took it out for its first long run, a four-and-a-half day flight. Even though it was just a test, the flight broke records for distance and endurance!

They tested and retested the airplane for 11,600 miles to work out all the initial problems. "Flying *Voyager*," remembers Dick, "was like riding on the back of an eagle." Jeana adds, "It rode like a sail-boat. It rocked and rolled like it was on the ocean." During the testing—for the first time in their lives—both pilots began to feel airsick. As they flew, the floor of the plane felt like concrete. With all the bumps and bangs, Dick and Jeana both became badly bruised. By the time they were done, Jeana respected *Voyager*, but Dick feared it. He had never been in an airplane that was so hard to fly.

Time to Go for It

At last, the big day came—December 14, 1986. Jeana and Dick knew that their chance was now or never. The flight was first planned for the middle of September, because the weather around the world

On December 14, 1986, Dick and Jeana decided to attempt their round-the-world journey. Cramped into a tiny cockpit, the team faced great uncertainty and dangers.

would be best. But there were many problems and delays. During one of the test flights, for example, part of *Voyager*'s front propeller fell off. Also, Jeana and Dick had tested the plane more than 60 times, but they had never taken off with a full fuel tank. As they stood by the plane that December, they realized that they had to go for it now, or wait another year for good weather. Dick felt that, at best, *Voyager* had a one-in-three chance of success. He feared that even a small problem could destroy the plane. But, despite the fears, he knew it was time. At dawn, Jeana and Dick put on cotton underwear, wool socks, fleece-lined moccasins, and their pale blue sweatsuits. They covered their shoelaces with gray tape so they would not catch on anything. Then the two pilots climbed into *Voyager.* Whatever the odds, it was now time for action.

Dick felt that at best, Voyager *had a one-in-three chance of success. Despite their fears, however, they both knew it was time.*

～ 5 ～

Courage and the Thrill
of the Unknown

E veryone involved knew that the *Voyager* flight was risky, but no one really realized just how dangerous the take-off could be. As the plane rolled down the runway, the ground crew ran along- side, holding the wing tips. Inside, Jeana and Dick were calm, but the people standing by were terrified. The wings were so loaded down with fuel that they scraped the runway. The plane could not pick up speed fast enough to take off. The ground crew radioed a frantic message to Dick in the cockpit, "Bring the stick back! Pull back!" Dick was so busy working the controls that he did not hear all of the message. Within seconds, he and the *Voyager* would run out of runway.

All of a sudden, the wings took flight. But the tops of the wings had broken off! The danger now was that one of the wings could pierce a fuel tank. Would Dick and Jeana have to turn back? Dick's brother Burt was following behind in another airplane. He actually wanted to ram his plane into *Voyager* to shake off the broken wing tips, but he knew that this would be much too dangerous. Fortunately, Dick was able to shake off the broken parts of the wings so the flight could go on.

Violent Storms Bring Great Danger

Voyager headed out to the Pacific Ocean. After a while, Dick and Jeana faced more danger as they flew over the Philippine Islands. There, the plane ran into a fierce tropical storm that swirled over an area of more than 600 miles. Winds of over 80 miles per hour slapped into the small vessel, as it tossed and turned like a leaf in a hurricane. Since Dick was the more experienced pilot, he stayed at the controls. He flew for 55 hours without a break. He did such a good job that Jeana did not fully realize the danger they had been in until much later. "I was never terrified until after the worst moments were behind us," she later said. But Dick knew how close they came to disaster. "It was like playing with fire," he remembers.

The storm had one good effect on the trip, however. Dick was able to ride on strong tailwinds, and the plane reached a speed of 147 miles per hour. This was about 50 miles over their average top speed. The faster they could go, the more distance they could travel and the more their chances of success improved. For a few moments after the storm, Dick and Jeana tried to relax.

Dick knew how close they had come to disaster. "It was like playing with fire," he remembers.

Because Jeana and Dick knew their survival depended on careful planning, they mapped out their route in great detail. But they had not counted on wild, dangerous storms. For much of their trip, Dick and Jeana had to fly higher than they had planned in order to get out of the raging weather. This strategy used up more of their precious fuel than they had expected. The severe weather affected the two pilots physically as well. As they plowed through the storms, Dick and Jeana suffered severe jolts and bangs as they rammed against the body of the plane.

Severe weather throughout the
journey threatened to destroy
Voyager and end the trip in
disaster.

More Peril

Furious storms were not the only danger Jeana and Dick faced. They also had to steer clear of Africa's high mountains. To avoid crashing, *Voyager* had to climb to 20,000 feet, which used up even more fuel. They also had to wear oxygen masks because *Voyager*'s cabin was not pressurized. Dick and Jeana were relieved once they made it through Africa's mountains safely. They thought that all the danger had now passed. But they were wrong.

Suddenly, the two pilots flew smack into a storm near the equator. For a second, Dick lost control of *Voyager*. Snapping into emergency action, he quickly got the airplane back on course. But what a close call it had been!

Trying to avoid dangerous storms and mountains took a lot of energy. Jeana and Dick were too busy to sleep, but they were also very tired. They were so tired, in fact, that they forgot to check the engine's oil. As a result, the back engine overheated and almost gave out. Their lack of sleep also made them unable to control their moods. One minute they felt happy; the next minute they felt scared. "We were on an emotional seesaw," Dick recalls.

There were still other problems to be faced. For one, it was very hard to eat and drink in the cramped little cockpit of the plane. During one of the test flights, Jeana had not had enough water and became sick. She knew that this time it was important to drink enough water.

After days of flying with little or no rest, Dick and Jeana became unable to control their moods.

Communicating with ground control was another big problem. *Voyager*'s small antenna made it hard to send and get radio messages. Many times, sounds came through, but the words could not be understood. Over and over, the ground crew asked Jeana and Dick to repeat their messages. After hours of straining to understand ground control, Dick got so angry that he simply stopped sending messages.

Triumph of Skill and Courage

Despite the many hazards and problems they faced, *Voyager* finally landed at Edwards Air Force Base in California on Tuesday, December 23, 1986, at 8:05 in the morning. Jeana Yeager and Dick Rutan had been in the air from December 14 to December 23.

On December 23, 1986, Jeana and Dick landed in California after being in the air for nine days and flying a total of almost 25,000 miles.

They had flown 24,987.727 miles and had set a new world's record for distance.

Once they were back on the ground, then-president Ronald Reagan awarded Jeana and Dick the Presidential Citizens Medal. This is a special award for people who have "performed exemplary deeds of service for their country or their fellow citizens." Today, *Voyager* hangs in the National Air and Space Museum in Washington, DC, right next to Charles A. Lindbergh's airplane, the *Spirit of St. Louis.* "Someday we may look back and see the Wright brothers to the present as one generation of airplane," said one aviation expert, "and *Voyager* to the future as a second."

By setting a world's record for distance, Jeana and Dick Rutan will have a special place in aviation history.

When Jeana and Dick greeted the press upon their safe arrival, one person asked them, "Was it worth it?" Without stopping a second to think, both pilots smiled and answered "yes" together. It was obvious to all who saw them that these two partners wouldn't have traded their adventure for anything in the world.

For their courage and great accomplishments, Jeana and Dick were awarded the Presidential Citizens Medal in 1986.

Chronology

1903   Orville Wright makes the first successful airplane flight.

1927   Charles A. Lindbergh becomes the first to fly alone across the Atlantic Ocean.

1932   Amelia Earhart becomes the first woman to cross the Atlantic by air.

1937   Amelia Earhart lost at sea.

1939   Dick Rutan born.

1947   Chuck Yeager breaks the sound barrier.

1952   Jeana Yeager born.

1962   Two Air Force pilots fly 12,532 miles on one load of fuel.

1976   Captain Eldon W. Joersz and Major George T. Morgan, Jr. set the world's speed record, 2,193 miles per hour.

1981   Dick and Jeana form their own aircraft firm, Voyager, Inc.

1984   *Voyager* construction completed.

1986   Dick Rutan and Jeana Yeager take off on *Voyager* for a trip around the world.

1986   *Voyager* sets a new world record for distance and non-stop flight.

Glossary

altitude Height from the ground to the air.

aviation The science of flight.

Communist A follower of communism, a political theory based on community ownership of all property.

convoys A group of military vessels that travels together.

drafting Drawing plans of machines or structures.

endurance Ability to last, continue, or remain.

engineering The science of putting scientific knowledge to practical use.

equator An imaginary circle that divides the Earth into the Northern and Southern hemispheres.

Fahrenheit A temperature scale.

insulation Any material that helps to prevent the passage or leakage of electricity, heat, or sound.

Mach number Number representing the ratio of an object's speed to a speed of sound in a specific environment.

navigator A person who charts a course.

obstacles Anything that gets in the way of a goal.

surveying Examining and inspecting land.

Further Reading

Berliner, Don. *Before the Wright Brothers.* Minneapolis, MN: Lerner, 1990.

————. *Distance Flights.* Minneapolis, MN: Lerner, 1990.

Grant, Donald. *Airplanes and Flying Machines.* New York: Scholastic, 1992.

Goold, Ian. *The Rutan Voyager.* Vero Beach, FL: Rourke, 1988.

Gunning, Thomas G. *Dream Planes.* New York: Macmillan, 1992.

Hook, Jason. *Twenty Names in Aviation.* North Bellmore, NY: Marshall Cavendish, 1990.

Levinson, Nancy S. *Chuck Yeager: The Man Who Broke the Sound Barrier.* New York: Walker, 1988.

Randolph, Blythe. *Charles Lindbergh.* New York: Watts, 1990.

Sabin, Louis. *Wilbur and Orville Wright: The Flight to Adventure.* Mahwah, NJ: Troll, 1983.

Seymour, Peter. *Pilots.* New York: Dutton, 1992.

Wade, Mary D. *Amelia Earhart: Flying for Adventure.* Brookfield, CT: Millbrook, 1992.

Williams, Brian. *Pioneers of Flight.* Madison, NJ: 1990.

Index